MEMOWARS OF A SCHIZOPHRENIC

MEMOWARS OF A
SCHIZOPHRENIC

R. van Niekerk

To order additional copies of this book, contact:
Xlibris Corporation
0-800-644-6988
www.xlibrispublishing.co.uk
Orders@xlibrispublishing.co.uk
304376

I hear voices in my head, they come to me, they understand, they talk to me, they understand, they talk to me and this is what they say: " I am the guided one."

Let me relate to you a story of a boy between the age of 5 and 8. Whose favourite program was bible stories. He use to watch this every Sunday, he never missed it almost like most people do with 7de laan now-a-days. Every Sunday the story was about a different prophet like Moses, David, Noah, Abraham and Jesus the son of Mary. I remember every Sunday when the boy watched that program he use to think "I wonder what it would be like to be a prophet, to make the blind see, to speak to different people's intellect, to proclaim the oneness of God the Creator, the One the Only, Firm Establish on the Throne of Authority." I think that was his biggest dream to work for the One the Only, the Creator, the Merciful, the One we all call God, Whom we all take for granted. Little did he know that the road he choose was not going to be easy, little did he know there would be some people who is going to love him, the message that he would preach and there would be others who would hate him and try to discredit, destroy and maybe even kill the poor little boy, kill him for speaking the truth from the Bible and the Holy Quraan.
So tell me on what side would you be? Would you love him or hate him? How and where do you find your Creator?

I remember how that young boy always searched for his Creator, the boy search high and low but he could never find what he was looking for until one day, or should I say one night, one dark night when he reach a low in his life and searched deep within his own soul. Have you ever reach that point in your life where you just do not care anymore? But what made the boy feel like that? What made him search within his own soul?

How do you judge a deed as good or bad? For example someone comes up to you and tell you if you do not do as he tells you:" your loved one's would be dead." What would you do? Would you break the law to protect the people you love? Or would you let them be killed? This is a lose, lose situation so what would you do if you where me in this kind of situation?

Let me tell you about the best country in the world. South Africa where human's have rights. Right number 1 freedom of speech just ask Julias Malema how often he practice that right? Running his mouth, scratching open old wounds, living in the past.
I must admit I do not blame him for thinking that way, for what the whites did to the so called coloureds and blacks in the apartheid era where there were boards posted along the beach that said "Strand and beach for whites only" and if you walked in a white area and the cops found you there (in that area) one of two things would happen. 1. They other beat you up drop you 10km from home and you must walk back to your house with your bruised body or 2. They arrested you and beat you up in the cells.

But now things have changed thanks to a great man called Mr. Nelson Mandela. Who learned me a great lesson do not fight fire with fire but show them you are better then them. I want to believe that, that man left a legacy behind. How else would we make this a better country Mr. Julius Malema?

Should we live in the past and get the whites back for what they did to our people or should we show them we are better? Why can't we just forget the past and built a better tomorrow. Can we change the past? Or should we learn from the past to make a better tomorrow.

What would happen to the youth if we filled their minds and hearts with so much anger? Would it be worth it? What happened to respect?

Have hatred made us so blind that we do not think of the future, the youth, our great nation and it's people. What happened to together we can do more? Or do you only use that catch phrase when you need my vote?

Can't we take all that anger and point it in a positive direction? When last did you take a drive through a poor community and see how the people live there and now I am speaking of personal experience how they beg for money, food, old clothes and broken shoes. Poverty is the order of the day.

So much misery in that kind of communities but do the politicians care? So much begging and poverty in that kind of communities but do the rich care? So many violence in that kind of communities but do the police care? Can somebody please tell me when will all of this change?

Where did we lose our way? What happened to caring about our neighbours? Don't we believe in God and his commandments anymore?

But enough about that let me tell you about Cape Town the mother city where everyday you hear" jou mase poes"

Some say this is the friendliest city in South-Africa where the people always smile and greet. Where you get treated with respect. Just on special occasions you will get a gun in your face and someone tells you "Money in the first bag, gold watches, earrings and bangles in the second bag, silver in the third bag and everything else in the fourth bag" That is just a joke don't be so sensitive. But let me tell you what makes this city so great.

In this city we have a little about everything like artists, comedians, sport stars, want to be gangsters who listen to much to 2pac, real gangsters, hustlers, killers, drug dealers almost like New York just a little better. Some would call it a concrete jungle others call it the land of opportunity. Where everybody worship the same dead thing called money.

Others chase women, cars, pipe dreams, broken dreams wondering when will I get there? This is not the movie "Are we there yet" so get of your ass, put that wineglass down, put the crack pipe (tikpype) down and work for your dream. Or take the easy way out and chase that dragon, drop that e (exticy) feel free for a couple of hours till you sober up and feel like shit. It is written every man shall have what he strives for. SO GET OFF YOUR ASS AND START WORKING.

In this life nothing is free. So why every time when I walk down the street and someone calls my name they always ask me for something, like money or a cigarette how can I pay for my own name.

Sports:

2010 Fifa soccer world cup was played where? Africa, South-Africa. The first game South-Africa verses Mexico I still remember it like it was yesterday, the first goal was scored by Siphewe Tshabala. The man who united a nation. The man who made you forget that you are black or white but who made you remember you are a South-African and proud of it. Proud of your country and how far you have come.

Bad luck boys for not making the second round but I hope our country can learn from that experience.
On the bright side we created two new records: the first host country who did not make it to the knock out stages, that's the negative one but the positive one which is also my favourite we won France for the first time in history the second proudest moment in the world cup.

There will be other world cups to set better records boys, so do not forget there are still African cup of nations that we can win and set a platform to reach the ultimate dream the world cup champs Bafana Bafana. Don't that sound lekka?

South Africans is a proud nation so we might not be the best in football, but what we lack in that department we make up in other sports departments like rugby. At the moment we are the best in rugby. The bulls super 14 champions. The Springboks the world cup champions for the second time since our debut on the international level. The most dominant team in rugby at the moment when last did you hear about the all blacks or wallabies? All you hear now-a-days on the rugby seen is the **mighty boks**.

Ask any South—African how proud is he/her about there rugby team? That was until the try nations when the all blacks made a come back. But we all know the all blacks and when the world cup come's.
What do they always do? Choke, almost like the Proteas our cricket team.

Our cricket team was also 1 of the best teams in the world in the time of Hansie Cronje but now that Graham Smith has taken over he plays for records and not trophies.

What I do not understand is if Graham Smith cares so much about records why did he call Hassim Amla off to declare when Hassim Amla was so close to braking his record in the 2009/2010 West-Indies-/India tour. Was that call personal or for the team cricket South-Africa?

Every time when our boys plays cricket and you get a Muslim guy along the road, in a shop and even on the golf course the first thing he asks always:" how much did Amla score?" The second thing:" is he still bating?" Hassim Amla the first Muslim, who plays for South Africa cricket, a hero or roll model to most young people, a man who was even called a terrorist by Shane Warne.

Muneeb Jospehs the first Muslim who played for Bafana Bafana. I hope that the Muslims are proud of you guys but unlike Muneeb Josephs Hasiem Amla refuse to play with a Castle Lager banner on his chest and for that the Muslims of South Africa stands behind you Sir Hassim Amla.

But my question is when will our cricket improve? When will we reach a semi-final in the cricket world cup again? When will they fire Graham Smith and get a new captain, someone with vision, someone who can take cricket to the next level, someone who leads by example who do not play for records or trophies but plays for respect when our team walks out on that pitch/field the opponent should fear us like they do Australia even though Matthew Hadden is not playing anymore.

When will our cricket team be one of the best in the world again and not just on paper? On paper we have a great team but when it comes to playing in big tournaments we just can not perform. So when will cricket South-Africa put the pride back in our team?

By the way thank you Graham Smith for not wanting to be the captain of the one day side anymore. You did a great job in the 2011 world cup. Can anyone tell me what was Graham Smith highest total that he scored? Is that not leading by example?

Media

The link of the world. The industry that can make you or brake you. 1. Ask Michael Jackson how the media crucified him, found him guilty before he even went to court. 2. Ask the Muslims how the media is discrediting them all over the world and making them out to be terrorists. O, how they love to spice up things.

The media can make you or brake you.

Just ask the people of Cape Town how a tabloid that you buy for R2 a day turned most of there children into drug users. Crystal Math was never famous until the arrival of that tabloid. Everyday, on the front page the story was about Crystal math. So youth that did not use drugs wanted to explore I mean when u read something in the newspaper is it not good? I guess it's true what they say:"sex, drugs and violence sells these days." But who cares how the money is coming in? As long as the money comes in we do not care how many lives we destroy.

When last did u read something good in the newspaper?

All you read these days: murder, drugs, rape, trails everything negative. How do you think does that negativity affect the minds of the people, the minds of the youth? No wonder violence, rape and murder increases in our neighbourhoods daily. So who can we blame except ourselves?

Why are we letting others dictate to us. Dictate on how to use our minds, dictate to us on how we should think and act. What happened to being independent, thinking for ourselves? When will we be free?

The mind that our Creator gave to us to reason between right and wrong. The same mind that makes us better then any other creation although we act like animals sometimes. The same mind that makes us the most honoured creation in the eyes of Our Creator. So why do we take that mind for granted and destroy it with drugs, alcohol and negative things? Use your mind be free, be independent and don't believe everything you read, everything you see and everything you hear.

When last did you read something positive in a newspaper? Or don't people do good anymore? Is disorder the order of the day? Or are the good people not news worthy? When will I read something positive again? Something that make me feel like a human, something that would make me feel like I have a heart, or is murder, rape, drugs the order of the day?

If we but only knew how that negativity is destroying our morals and our humanity. We use to be brothers and sisters now we are bastards and bitches. So who do we blame?

Why do we buy the tabloids? For the news, for the gossip or do we buy it to have a good look at page 3? Look at how they are exploiting and arousing the lust in men. Look at how they are using our lust against us to make money. Are we not Stupid, men? Do men always think with the wrong head?

Television and Soaps

When u walk around 6.30 pm in my neighbourhood u will not find a soul outside. Everybody is in front of there televisions watching 7de laan. What makes us watch this soapy?

I guess we all love the drama, the friendships, the closeness where a community sticks together and fight for what is right. Do you remember when Geeta wanted to change the heights and wanted to put all the tenants out on the street? How they all stood together and fought for what is right?

When last did our communities stick together for something that is right? I guess we all watch 7de laan to remind us of what our communities use to be like. Loving, caring looking out for each other.

Now we live like strangers building high walls between us. Drug dealers and sherbeens (brothels) open daily and we don't care. It is like we have given up on life. Do we ever think for a second about our kids, about the future and how this would destroy them in future years? Where did we go wrong? Will we ever get that closeness back? Drugs and wine move in and our morals move out.

Can anyone tell me where can I find a wife like Charmain (from 7de laan) that stands by her husband for better or worst, in richer and poorer, threw sickness and health, a shoulder to cry on, someone who catch u when u fall, who picks you up when you are down . These days that kind of women are hard to find.

Soaps like days of our lives, Gossip Girl and bold and beautiful got teenagers thinking sex before marriages is right. Did we forget about the 10 commandments? That's why most of the girls want to act like whores and they wonder why we call them bitches.

Be a man because real men do not hit women just sometimes when she provokes you, or when you are drunk, or when you need money to support your drug habits, or when she acts like a slat, or when she is drunk. No matter how you look at it real men do not hit women and that one advertisement don't help either.

That one love life advertisement do not help either. The one where the two teenagers with their school clothes on is having sex in the classroom. Do you know that advertisement? Did you ever see it before?

What is that telling the children in our schools? What is that telling the youth who is suppose to be the leaders of tomorrow? To have sex at that age is all right, to sleep around is all right. Parents isn't that what that advertisement is telling our kids? So when will the parents stand up for what is right?

How about they change that advertisement to were the girl tells the guy "I am not ready for sex or put a ring on this finger then you can have all of me." The best gift you can give your husband is your purity. Who would appreciate it more then him? Be one of a kind say" No." or do you want the guys to make fun of you calling you Easy?

Did you notice almost every second advertisement on television is about alcohol plus that advertisement is so attractive, it makes the wine look so delicious, it makes your mouth water. After that advertisement you have an instant need to drink, did you ever notice that if you are a drinker? Did you ever notice how advertisements creates needs? No wonder most of the shebeens sells alcohol to under 18's. Can we not see how wine and drugs destroys homes, families and communities? Are we that blind?

But in the modern day society if you do not drink or do not do drugs then you are not cool.
Is that why most teenagers now-a-days drink and do drugs? To be cool because cool rule even though you are messing up your lives.

Be cool stay in school, go to university, make something of your life. Can you not see so many broken homes are there in your area? There is only one way to survive make something with your life, go against the odds. Make the right choices, be different.

Who cares for you but yourself and your family? But do not listen to them be one those who kill there parents to please there friends!

Life is not easy but always be true to yourself do not let them back you up, smack you up and even drug you up be strong. Stand up for what you believe in don't be backed into a corner, speak out don't let they shut you up, don't let other people be the cause of you doing drugs, believe in yourself. If you ever need some help drop to your knees and pray but don't do that . . . .

Be a coward take the easy way out, drink that alcohol take that drugs, put a gun against your head and blow out your brain. Always remember a true friend is someone who encourage good and prohibit bad.

MOVIES

Hollywood I have a great idea for a couple of movies. Movies that would debut at number one all across the world. But let me tell you about it. 1st movie: the name" Global Terror" what a name. doesn't that sound like a sure winner? Let me tell you more about this movie. A man lets call him the Magdie. This Magdie stands for right, equality, fairness etc. and this Magdie's 1st order of business is to unify the Muslims all over the world. 2nd this Magdie approaches the media and want to clear all the negative stuff that they are saying about Muslims being terrorists. 3rd this Magdie approaches the leader of the free world and want to come with some sort of truce about the September 11th attack, the invasion on Afghanistan & Iraq and the camps where the Americans are keeping the so-called terrorists hostage.

But round about here the movie starts getting tricky because he and the president of the United States don't see eye to eye and they can not come to some sort of an agreement.
So what do you think will happen next?

All hell breaks out but this time the rules of the game chance because this time all the Muslims is on one page and stands behind the Magdie.

So if the Magdie says jihad "holy war" the Muslims follow without any hesitation. So what will happen next to show the world how serious the Magdie is he sets demands and deadlines. Since America do not deal with terrorists and there demands the Magdie give the order to let some buildings be bomb. Buildings like the empire state building and the stature of Liberty in New-York.

Now all hell breaks loose because America retaliates. But this war will get ugly because this war would make the September 11th attack look like a joke, this time the whole of America will be under attack, this time instead of America invading Afghanistan or Iraq it will be the opposite.

This time it will be America who will be invaded. Imagine that . . . . America in chaos. Don't you think people would pay money to see that? How many countries would love to see that?

Plus there is a bonus to this movie because this movie can be made three ways

1. Where America wins the war.
2. Where the Magdie wins the war
3. Where they work out a truce and both parties walk away happy.

Don't you think this movie would be better then' Inglorious Bastards" where some Jews can't get over the fact that Hitler killed so many of them.

They can't get him back in real life so they do the second best thing get him back in a movie. Can't they move on and forget. What if I should tell them that maybe I know where Hitler is buried and for the right price I can tell you.

2nd movie. A disaster movie, "Armageddon" and not even Bruce Willis can stop this one. Imagine lava boiling from the earth, the mountains getting rolled up like a lawn (grass), the sea putting forth waves bigger then what happened in Tahiti, imagine the terror how would the people run around calling on there Creator then to top all that imagine the sun and moon colliding the scattered pieces falling down to earth, imagine the chaos. Now imagine how the end of creation would be? When gravity is taken a way? This time there will not be the day after tomorrow. Do you think that such a kind of movie would make money?

3rd movie last but not least we could just make a movie about a crazy man who wants to change the world, make it a better place for the future generations to come.

Can someone please tell me why is only in the movies happy endings? When will I get my happily ever after like Shrek ?

IDOL WORSHIPPING

What is idol worshipping? Let's go back, back into time when people did not believe in a Creator. A time when people believed in the sun, the moon and disorder was the order of the day. So the Creator, the Almighty different from creation send prophets to guide man, guide man to protect them against themselves.

Look at the time when Faro the king of Egypt used the Jews as slaves. So what did the Creator do? The Creator send help in the form of Moses to guide his people to the promise land. But what did this people of Moses do? After they saw all the favours that the All Mighty did for them like leading them through the red sea, I mean they saw with their own eyes how the red sea opened and give them a path to walk through.

What did that ungrateful people do? Are we like that sometimes? Ungrateful.

When Moses went up to the mountain where he received the 10 commandments. Let me tell you what that ungrateful people did. They built a calf made of gold. I mean this people saw the favours of the All Mighty Creator with there own eyes and yet they rejected it. Are we like that sometimes?

After God has help us through a hard time we reject. We reject the Creator who took care of us when we were in the bellies of our mothers, Who give us fresh oxygen, Who give us the strength to get out of bed ever morning to go earn a living but yet when that same God speaks we turn our backs and choice the live of this world forgetting when we die we must return to were we came from.

Look at the time of the prophet Abraham when the people believed in the sun what did the prophet Abraham do? He said I believe in the sun but when night came and the sun was gone he asked where is my creator now? He then said he can not believe in a creator that disappear so then he said I believe in the moon and stars and when the day came again and the moon and stars disappear what did he do? Then one day when they left the prophet Abraham alone to look after some of the idols, do you know what he did? He took an axe and smashed all the idols but left the biggest one and put the axe around his neck.

When his people returned and ask him what happened his answer was ask the idol. What is the lesson in there for us to learn from?

Let us go back to the time of Sodom and Gomorrah where disorder like prostitution, men sleeping with men woman sleeping with woman was the order of the day. Today we call it gay rites. What happened to that people? The Creator destroyed them and there city. When last did the Creator destroy a city or nation?

Now-a-days we destroy ourselves with diseases like aids, drugs, wars etc. Look in America how often is there disasters like tornados or lest take some of the recent one's Tahiti or Sonoma is that the Creator giving us signs and telling us that the end of the universe is close or is that just nature? But what is idol worshipping and are we at present time guilty of that?

Tell me parents what posters do yours kids have on there walls, in there rooms? Do your kids dress and act like that person on that poster? So can you say with an honest heart that your kids did not lose there ways?

If you do not believe me you should check out the internet like facebook and see for yourself the kind of picture that your kids post online. While you on that you should also check out mxit and see what kind of conversations your kids have.

To top all this look in our churches is there idols? Look in our homes, is there photos of Jesus? Do we really know what Jesus looked like? I bet if

Jesus should return now we all would reject him for one simple reason, if he do not look the same like in the pictures we have in our homes and the idols we have in our churches. Isn't praying to an idol the same as idol worshipping? Isn't that the same what people of the past did? Have we forgotten the 1st commandment? I guess that is why the pastors at present time break away and start there own churches.

MUSIC

What would life be without music? Jazz, pop, rock, r & b, love songs and my favourite gangster rap. Music is always there to help you through bad times, pick you up when you are down and when you are in love what kind of music do you listen to? So there is different music for different times. .

Did you ever notice that the kind of music that a person listen to tells you the kind of mood that, that person is in. One of my dreams is to make an album with Andre Young aka Dr. Dre the father of rap. Some of my favourite artists is 2pac, 50cent, but now that Lil Wayne stepped on the scene the Rasta Farions have been getting more women then me. Laugh that's a joke don't be so sensitive that's a good song but really ever since that hit came out the Rasta Farions have become very popular. Do not forget Snoop Dogg, Jay Z, Akon.

This question is for all the kids who listen to these different artists. Why do you worship these artist? When they are as human as you? Only difference between you and them is they are famous you are not. But did you ever ask yourself:" why are they famous?" Could it be that unlike you they didn't give up on there dreams?

Did you ever study their lives? Who of their lives are perfect? Ask Maria Carrey how her marriages is after she provoke Eminem in that song obsession?

Do you know what Eminem did? Let me tell you what that man did. He made a song called "the warning "you should listen to both that songs. I wonder what Maria Carrey's husband did after hearing all of that?

But I must say if my wife had a voice like Maria Carrey she can sing me every night to sleep and when she sing that song "I want to know what love is" I would fall in love with her all over again and make twins.

I wonder how Rihanna is after Chris Brown transformed her face and turned that song into a hit "I can transform you." Ask 50 how he feels every time when Jay-z dismiss him in a song? Ask Jay-z how he felt when 2pac use to dismiss him? Now Jay-z is the self proclaimed best rapper alive that's before I will step on the scene. I wonder why did Beyonce one of the top divas cry on the Tyra Banks show when she sang :I wish I was a boy"? if you needed a shoulder to cry on I've got two.

So tell me all of you who listen to 2pac "hit them up" tell me why do you think that you are a hardcore gangster after you listened to that song? Let me do one better if you were 2pac and you were five times what would you have done?

I know what I would have done, I would have wanted revenge. Wouldn't you want the same thing Revenge? But what would revenge mean, gang violence, death, murder.

But what did 2pac do? He made that into a song and made a lot of money with it. So isn't that a sign that we aren't 2pac we can't do what he did we can't think like he did. So if you want to be like 2pac take all that anger and point it in something positive.

Did you ever listen to the message that 2pac is trying to convey in his music? Let me tell you, you wane be 2pac what does he say about drug dealing/drug dealers:" you make money in a sleazy way" revering to the song "Chances" meaning you make money the wrong way but why would a hardcore gangster like 2pac say this?

Do you drug dealers ever look at what you are doing to your community? How can you make money at the expense of other peoples misery? Instead of building the community you are breaking it down, praying on others weakness. Encouraging them to kill, steal what other honest people work so hard for and sell it for next to nothing just to get a quick fix of something they think they need. Why do we destroy ourselves? How can we destroy our own kind? Have you ever seen a drug addict? How does he or she look?

So when will the community stand up and vote these people out. These people are taking away your kids, they are taking away the future and in return what do they give you? Death, families breaking up, violence just to mention a few. So what is the answer? When will we stand together black, white, coloured, rich and poor. Just because your kid don't do drugs now wont say that he/she wont do it in the future, what about your grandchildren? Or don't we ever think about tomorrow?

So drug dealers who listen to 2pac what do you have to say?

Or maybe we should ask government to legalize drugs then at least government would have a say in the most profitable business these days.

So to all the gangsters who listen to 2pac. I wonder what does 2pac have to say about that "mad at the world because you came from a broken home . . . . tell me if you die let me know will heart feel pain watching as your mother cry will all your homies ride or will they get high and talk about how you died": from the song "lil homies" so what is the message that this great man is trying to convey?

Did you become a gangster because you are mad at the world and things in your house are not right? Maybe its poverty, maybe you grow up with out a father? What ever it is I do not want to judge you. Who am I to judge if I am just as mortal as you?

A man who's life is not perfect, but a man who want to see a change, a man who want to see his brothers and sisters survive, who is tired of seeing how his brothers kill each other because they are not from the same area or same gang. Can anyone tell me what are you fighting for or about?

Today killing is so easy just take a gun and squeeze the trigger or take a knife and stab. The hardest thing is to walk away and forgive. How would your friends see you if you do that?

How would your friends judge you if you do that and just walk away? I can hear how you are running your mouths and saying you are weak. But what would you do if someone wants to kill you? What would you do if someone shoots at you?

I have seen gangster get religious when they start bleeding screaming:" Lord help me. "I have seen killers begging for there lives. What would you do if that was you?

You know what I do not understand this is like a cycle, history repeating itself, kids look but they do not see the life of a gangster always looking over your shoulder, always carrying a gun or a knife, being paranoid all the time because in your eyes someone is always out to get you. Gangster know what kind of life's do you have so why do you want someone else in that same kind of predicament?

Don't we want to see others happy? Or are we so caught up in that life fast cars, flashy rings, women drooling over you. We do not take the time to judge ourselves? Can we ever change? Is there another life better then the one we are having now? Or am I to selfish to give someone else a better life then the one that I am having now? Is the life I am having now truly the life I wanted? What is change? Or is it to late for me to change? If you only know what we are doing . . . killing our own kind no wonder you must go to sleep every night high.

I heard some gangster boasting about who have the biggest heart. Do you truly know what that means? Why do you have a heart?

Wasn't your heart created to feel emotions? So if you say you have the biggest heart doesn't that mean that you have the biggest emotions? What would joy be without pain? So if you say you have the biggest heart doesn't that mean that if you are in hell you will not drag someone else down into hell with you?

But you would protect him/her, guide him/her not to make the same mistakes you made in your life? Would that not put a smile on your face knowing you helped someone to make a success of his/her life? Did you ever check yourself gangster? Did you ever check when last did you smile? All these years watching my friends and seeing how they are throwing there lives away into drugs and gangsterism got me praying for better days, better ways. But since it looks like the lord are not hearing my prayers it is up to me to safe who is willing to listen because it is written we do not chance conditions unless you chance it yourselves.

There will be hard times in front of you, with many tests, people who will be trying to divert you off the path of chasing your dreams to make a better life for you and your family. But I beg you do not be like most of the guys that I grew up with who slip, fall and can not get up.

The road is hard and long so if you should slip or fall get up dust yourself off and proceed you do not need weed to succeed. A line yourself with people who care about you, who wants you to succeed in this world filled with greed. Who can you trust? But yourself always follow your instinct cause even in the hood true homies make you fell good. True friends will help you up. They will not step on you when you are down. In my life I have seen straight A students throwing their lives because they wanted to be cool they tried drugs once and they were hooked. I have seen guys with raw talent who could have played for the Stormers rugby or for the cobras cricket threw there lives away for following fake friends or for giving in to there needs and pure pressure.

I just don't want you to do the same. My Lord please hear me:" guide this people to a better life." Always remember you are not better then other people show mercy, act better then they do and if someone should break your heart except she wasn't the one for you get better. Don't go for 1st come 1st serve.

Someone who would stand by your side threw the hard times, someone who can put a smile on your face, someone who would catch you when you fall who will be there through it all, a shoulder to cry on, an ear to listen. Someone who isn't selfish because your dreams are her dreams and her dreams is yours.

So Dr. Dre or should I call you Andre Young back to you about my 1st album that I want you to produce I call it "The Arrival". I want to work with you because you are the best. The man who gave us the od's, eezee ees, ice-cubes, doc's the Snoop Dogg's, and the group who said fuck the police and I wont do you like some people after you turned a 50cent into 50 million sold world wide. Here is some lyrics for my 1st single;

> I am the best all the way from the western cape,
> land of the grape vine where woman are fine
> I think Beyonce is devine almost like our best wine,
> ain't no man as crazy as me, Fuck jay-z
> I don't do drugs but ill fill your ass up with slug's heart of
> a soldier ain't no man colder but baby you can cry on my
> shoulder.
> In this world of greed a man who wants to succeed don't need
> weed, but I'll make you feel like you are on speed.

Chorus: however do you want it, however do you need it, however do you want it however do you need it, cape-town the mother city better then brooklyn and jozi

Little homie like a bird and you aim so high, wishing you could fly to reach your dreams
stay away from the crocked sceams, ain't nothing worst then shatterd dreams.
get your mindset right stay focus study hard and if ever you should slip or fall I will be there through it all.
Don't need a gang to hang don't need to be cool but stay in school don't be cruel to rule always help those in need. Proceed without weed you are the last of the Don breed. Roxy Louw is hot what's this spot Ja-rule is a fool.

Chorus:

past crimes hard times got me on my knees
begging: Lord please: in this right man's world we are always wrong had to remain strong to prove them wrong. Payback is a bitch I want to be rich. Who is laughing now. After ever darkness there is light remain bright can no body stop my shine that's why I stay on the grind
if you look for me I ain't that hard to find I always have an Ak 47 so ill send you to hell of heaven your choice homie so Nicky Minaj are you a sweet dream or a beautiful nightmare

Chorus:

Always remember an artist is someone who relates his/her life to you threw a song so next time when you listen to a song don't just listen to the chorus but listen to the message in that song.

LOVE

What is the definition of love? Two in bed trying to make three. Where I cum from love have different meanings. You will find a guy or girl who says they love you but every time when that person is drunk she makes out/ have sex with someone else. Is that love?

Or someone when you have a car she sits left front but when you don't have a car anymore she says bye-bye. Is that love?

How about when you are sick or end up in hospital she don't even come visit you once. When you look for her she is busy partying and you are the last thing on her mind.
Love is blind and it will take over your mind. Does true love still exist?

Why don't we take a relationship were the guy tell his girlfriend that he loves her but then you see her walking around she will have a black eye. What would you call that?

Do you remember how it feels to fall in love? Isn't that the best feeling in the world? So why when someone breaks your heart, why do you feel so helpless? So worthless? Why do we feel that we just want to give up? Why do we turn to drugs, wine to mend our broken hearts? Is there a better way to mend our broken hearts?

Don't we understand that it isn't love that did that to us. We just fell in love with the wrong selfish, ungrateful person. To all the young girls love isn't about opening your legs. Love never gave up on us we gave up on love. Do you remember how a broken heart feels like?

I wish there is something I could say to make the pain go away. If you want to cry go ahead and cry maybe it will make you feel better. I know it is not easy to pick up the pieces of your broken heart, all that dreams you had for each other. Gone. All the plans you had for each other. Gone. What to do next? Do you believe in yourself? Do you believe some where out there someone is waiting to love you unconditionally?

What if that person that broke your heart is not for you? Do you believe in soul mates? Don't let someone else make you feel bad, you are beautiful, you are special, you are one of a kind. You are a survivor. I know it is hard but you can do it, look deep with in yourself, don't you still have a lot of love to give to that special person, that person who will make your knees jelly (weak), your heart beat faster, your palms sweaty and makes your smile bigger. So why do you feel so down? When you have so much to life for. Dust yourself off and get up.

So remember take the good leave the bad and learn from your mistakes. Don't fall in love with someone who is selfish or will take you for granted. To be in love, isn't that the best feeling in the world? So those of you who found their soul mates love them, treat them with kindness, respect and tell them, show them through your actions how you feel about them every day. Don't ever take them for granted, in this world today true love is hard to find. To those who is still waiting on their prince or princess to come and rescue them, keep the faith be patient he will come guess I am just a hopeless romantic.

PARENTHOOD

Do you remember how it felt when the baby kick inside your stomach, mothers? How about the fathers do you remember how it felt the baby kick when you put your hand on the stomach on your wife or girlfriend? How did it feel when you hold your baby for the 1st time in your arms? Do you remember all the promises you made that day? So what changed?

How can a mother leave her child? What kind of mother leaves her baby to be raised by his father? How can a father rape his own child? How can a mother hold her own baby between 3 and 9 years old down so her boyfriend can rape the baby? Can someone please explain that to me. Where did we go wrong?

What kind of mother would leave a 8 year old to look after a 2 year old while she is getting drunk? When you look at your child what do you see? Don't you want to give your child everything you never had? But lately it looks like if you can't have your dreams you might as well take your kids down with you.

Or is it easier to make someone pregnant and leave her? Do you know what it is like to grow up without a father? So why do you want to do the same thing to your own blood, don't you want to be better then your father who left you and your mother? How would you like it if your child call someone else daddy or mummy?

I thought it is our job as parents to protect our kids? Lately it looks like we hurt them more.
Then you get the parent who's children are angels. Their children do nothing wrong, it is always their friends. Someone gets robed everybody sees it is your child who did it but you still say it isn't my baby. It is always other people but never your kids. Are you like that? In the house our kids are angels but the moment that child leaves the house they turn into devils. So when will parents wake up and smell the coffee.

Or you get the parent who breaks his kids spirit, who destroys his kid mentally. This kind of parent have never anything nice or positive to tell his kids. He never sees the good in his kids. They always say to their kids: "you are a fuck up" don't you ever think what that words can do to your kids? Aren't we the ones to whom our kids look up to, aren't we the ones that must lift our children's spirits when they are down?

Or are our lives fucked up and we take the anger out on our kids. In the past the Arabs use to bury there 1st born (if it was a girl) alive. Are we that different? Or are we worst? Do we kill our children today?

Aren't children suppose to be a blessing so why do we treat them like a curse? There are some people who would give anything to have a child even adopt. So why do so may teenagers today commit legal murder? When they could make someone else happy, when they could let someone else adopt their child. Why do we kill the future?

THE UNSEEN

Watching to much of supernatural got you believing that you can see demons, vampires, shape shifters etc. do these things really exist?

VAMPIRES:

Is a thing that suck out your blood right? A parasite? So let me ask you this. Did you ever had friends or a girlfriend, every time when you have money they cling to you just like a parasite? As soon as that money is gone they vanish leaving you high and dry.

SHAPE SHIFTERS:

Is a thing that change shape almost like a chameleon change their colour. So tell me did you ever have a friend or friends when they are with you they talk bad about other people? So tell me what if that friends is with other people will they not talk bad of you?

DEMONS:

Is an evil spirit. So tell me did you ever had friends or a voice in your head every time when you want to do good that voice or so called friends tell you not to? Or did you ever have people forcing you to do something against your will? Something that kills your inner self, that makes you fell like u are not a man. They kill your dignity.

HELLHOUNDS

Did you ever dream about a dog/s that where chasing you in your dreams and no matter how hard you run you just couldn't get away from them? Remember this it is your dreams anything is possible in your dreams, if you want them dead you can kill them. Don't let nothing stand between you and reaching your dreams.

WAREWOLVES

Did you every know a young, innocent lady as soon as the moon comes out her innocence go a way. What I mean is as soon as she is drunk or full of drugs she chance into a nymph.

Are there things in this world that we refuse to see? Do you believe in the unseen? How about angels? Do you believe in that? How about God? Do you ever ponder who God your Creator is?

Are you amongst those who believe what the white man told you that god is weak? Can the Creator be different from creation? How about a baby, how can a baby who don't know about sin be born with sin? Wouldn't it better if we say that the new born inherits the sins of the world.

In this world everybody lies but you must always be one step ahead of them. Don't hear what they tell you but watch there actions that never lies. Prepare for the worst and wish for the best.

What if God our Creator is All around us? What if you can study Your Creator through what He the Almighty has created? What if God the One the Only is different from what he has created? Could this be possible?

CHANGE:

What is change? Did you ever ask yourself why am I a Christian or Muslim? Aren't most of us the religion that we were born into? Did we ever take the time to investigate if our believe is for real and that the white man didn't tamper with our bible or believes?

What is change and why are humans so afraid of change? If a drug addict can go to rehab and a criminal go to prison to get rehabilitated what is wrong with you? Don't you believe in yourself? Have you given up on yourself? Isn't change to have a different outlook on life.

Not to take anything for granted but to appreciate what you have, to work hard for what you want, never give up on yourself, fight for what you want for what is right, not to do what you use too, educate yourself because knowledge is power, remember that, to learn from your past mistakes because what don't kill you makes you stronger, get money don't get tempted, get your mindset right believe in a higher power, always stay humble, don't worry to much about people who judge you let them judge themselves show them the middle finger.

Did you ever notice it is easier to move backwards in life, to go from good to bad, to go from sober to drunk and high. So why change when all your friends are getting drunk and getting high? Isn't that better then studying or going to church besides if you don't drink and get high you will be treated like an outcast. Who wants to be treated that way?

So go mess up your life but don't come crying when 5years from now, you are a bum and you see your friends driving expensive cars while you are riding a bicycle.

Life is all about choices you made your bed now lie in it. Always remember it is never too late to swallow your pride admit when you are wrong and find a better way before death comes knocking at your door. Death don't ask for age, show me anyone you know who cheated death.

People ask me if there is still racism in South-Africa all I can tell you is the white still look out for the whites, the blacks still look out for the blacks and the coloureds still stab each other in the back. Before we get to believe where we all will ask the pope who rewrote the bible lets make a quick detour.

America

Congratulations Mr. Barack Obama the 1st black president. What a great honour but with great power comes a great responsibility, how I wish I was a reporter so I can ask you a few questions: Is there still racism in your country? How is the white man coping with the fact that America the land of the free have a black president?
My reason for asking this, some of my friends have down loaded some footage from the internet.

It is called the Barack Obama conspiracy it is dangerous footage: "they say you are not a man of your word, you say one thing and do another" like a few years ago you said that president Bush was wrong to invade Afghanistan and Iraq but now you are doing the same. Do the white man hate you that much president Obama?

They also say that you (president Bush and president Clinton before you) are working for The Bulderberg Group. Do the white man hate you that much?

They say that the Bulderberg group is a group who own wall street that this peoples agenda is to control the world financially that's why the dollar never drop and this people is responsible for the September 11th attack.

So why blame the Muslims? Is it because all of them look like each other with there long beards, dresses and that things on there heads," O, how I wish I was one of them" and there women look so beautiful everything covered except there hands and faces.

It looks like these people who made this documentary is making me believe them president Obama. If they can put a doubt in my head how many others across the world have watched this footage already and how many lost there faith in you sir? I want to believe you when you say that you "are from krypton came to save planet earth." Please proof these people wrong president Obama. I just wanted to warn you and inform you about this President Obama.

BELIEVE:

What is believe? A wise man once told me believe can move mountains. Would I be wrong to put our believes, the Holy Bible and the Holy Quraan to the test because there are people out there like scientist who do not believe in a Creator. So let's see if I can proof to myself that our believe have no flaws and maybe we will have some answers for the scientists' like Darwin who said that the human race started with some cells that come from the sea. Maybe his mom was as big as a whale.

I am sure you would not mind if we use logic.
So let's start with the bible:

God created us in his own image. So does that mean we look like god? In another verse were God spoke to Moses didn't God appear as a burning bush? Now I am confused if god created us in his image why can't I turn into a burning bush? So let us ask the question if God the Creator created shape is He then in need of shape?

Do we truly believe that God the Powerful is weak? The bible says that Satan is trying to overthrow god. So tell me if God the Eternal created Satan couldn't that same Creator, The Most Powerful destroy Satan? Think about this for a second isn't that an insult to God? Or how about after when God created the heavens and the earth in 6 days he rested. Does that mean God gets tired? Then all this time I have been worshipping a weak god. No wonder men think that they are gods.

I mean a god who gets tired, a god who's creation is stronger then him. Maybe I should change my believe and worship Satan. But what if . . . .

What if . . . . God the Creator the All Powerful is not like what He the Exalted has created. What if God the Great is different from his creation? Is this possible, can God the All Mighty be different from what He has created? Open your mind for a second and think about this.

Now let's see if Jesus is the son of God. Where in the bible does Jesus say in his own words that he is the son of God and I am not talking about someone else who's words is a looting to that I mean where Jesus says in his own words that he is the son of God the creator. When Satan come to Jesus the son of Mary and said to Jesus to worship him. What did Jesus answer him? What would you have answered if you were the son of the Creator? I know I would have told Satan I am the son of god why should I worship you but what did Jesus answer?

Let me tell you what did Jesus answer:" there are written that I should worship one God" and when the lady grabbed his thobe and said "o merciful one" what did Jesus tell her : "the One who sent me is Merciful" how about when the high priest ask Jesus if he was the son of god what did Jesus answer him: "you say I am the son of god" if Jesus was the son of god what would his answer be? Wouldn't he have said I am the son of god? Did you ever think of this before?

So would it be safe to say that Jesus is the son of Mary and was send to the lost tribe of Israel. This part I do not understand if Jesus was send to the lost tribe of Israel why do we claim we are Christians? When Jesus was not send to us.

So why don't the Christian leaders answer the bible scholars when they ask these questions about the bible. How about I add another few questions of my own.

Like why was some parts of the bible only written +-80 years after the death of Jesus? Who didn't eat with Jesus, who didn't talk to Jesus, who wasn't a disciple of Jesus and why some scriptures starts with according to?

Do you know what according to me? According to Jennifer, Alice had sex with Richard. According to is the words people use when they want to gossip about other people. I do not understand why don't our people study history. Let me give u another fact. When Jesus the son of Mary was hanging on the cross he said: "O Lord why do Thee forsake me" now do that sound like the son of the Lord?

But however the Lord of the Worlds is Great and truly Merciful if Marcus could see a vision on his way to Damascus and he the Lord the Merciful to forgive him what is wrong with you and me. Do you know what he did before he saw that vision, that man was a bounty hunter who hunted Christians for cash and he still wrote part of the Bible. So did you ask yourself how merciful is our Lord really?

If our Lord the Great can forgive him what is wrong with me and you who committed patty crimes and sins. So drop to your knees and ask for forgiveness for all the sins we have committed. Who of us in this world is sinless? Do you remember what Jesus said to the people who wanted to stone the prostitute?" let he who don't have any sin cast the first stone" so why do we discuss other peoples lives when our lives is not sorted out, when we have more problems then others? Or is that the way we hide our flaws?

So let's go to the most read book in the world today the Holy Quraan and see what this holy book say.

Did you know that almost every second Muslims in the world today have memorized the Holy Quraan, so if the enemies of Islam should burn all the Holy Quraan's in the world the Muslims can produce a new Holy Quraan within a week to the Muslims this book is direct from there Creator Allah that was revealed to there prophet Mohammad (peach and blessings upon him) it was recorded and written in his time and preserved until today and up till the end of time. So lets see if they are right if this book is from there Lord Allah the One the Only, the Most Powerful. What do we know about Islam except to what the media is telling us.

Do we ever take the time to study and try to understand that maybe there are another reason why the enemies of this perfect way of life want to destroy them. Lets take some verse of this Holy Quraan and put it to the test for those who reject the existence of a Creator:" look at the creation of the Lord and see for yourself if there is any flaws, look a second time and see if you can find any flaws" did you ever look up at the sky and see if there is any flaws? If you don't find any flows the 1st time Allah the Merciful challenge you a 2nd time to look. Is it not created perfected?

So next time when you look up at the sky look and ask this question if this was created perfect how perfect is our Creator, beyond the beyond and far beyond the beyond, free from all want and need. So lets study there Creator, however the Muslims assign 20 attributes to there Creator.

Allah Himself, without beginning, without an end, different from creations, independent in Existence, oneness(unity that don't consists of any parts), power, will, knowledge, life, hearing, sight, speech, omnipotent (all powerful), willer (He who wills), omniscient (all knower), alive, hearer He who hears), seer (He who sees), speaker (he who speaks) with 99 beautiful names like Allah, The Compassionate, The most Merciful, The Sovereign, The Holy One Who is Free from All Blemishes, The Giver of Peace or One who Immune From All Distresses, The Guardian of Faith, The Giver of Protection, The Mighty, The Overpowering Lord, The Self-Glorious, The Creator, The One Who Gives Life, The Fashioner of Shapes, The Exceedingly Forgiving, The One Who Has Control Over All Things, The Giver of All Things, The Sustainer and Provider, The Remover of Difficulties and Giver of Decisions, The All Knowing, The Straightener of Sustenance, The Extender of Sustenance, The Abaser-The One Who Humbles and Lowers, The Exalter, The Giver of Honour, The Giver of Dishonour, The All-Hearing, The One Who Sees All Things, The Maker of Immutable Judgements, The Just, The Most Affectionate or Knower of Innermost Secrests, The All Informed, The Clement, The Great, The Forgiving, The Highly Grateful, The Most High, The Most Great or Infinite, The Protector, The Giver of Strength, The Reckoner, The Glorious, The Benevolent, The Caretaker, The Answerer of Prayers, The Lenient, The Wise, the Most Loving, The Most Venerable, The Resurrector of the Dead, The Omnipresent, The Truth, The Provider, The Almighty, The Invincible, The Patron, The Praiseworthy, The Keeper of Counts, The Originator, The

One Who Has the Power To Create A Gain, the Giver Of Life,
The Giver of Death, The Everlasting, The Sustainer of Life, The
All-Perfect, The All-excellent And The One With Veneration,
The One Or The One Unequalled,

The One Free From All Want, The All Powerful, The
Power(Creator Of Power), The One Who Causes Advancement,
the One Who Causes Retardation, The First, The Last, The
Obvious, The Latent, The One Who Exercises Responsibilities
Over All Things, The One Far Above The Attributes Of Entire
Creation, The Good, The Oft Returning, The One who takes
Retribution, The One Who Pardons, The Kind, The Possessor
of Sovereignity,

The Majestic and Benevolent, The Just, The Assembler, The
One Free From All Need, The Supplier of Need To Others, The
Hinderer, The One who can cause loss, The One Who Confers
Benefits, The Light, The One Who Gives Guidance, The
Deviser, The Eternal, The Supporter of All(that is good) Or The
One Who Remains Alive Even after Everyone And Everything
Dies, The One Who Guides Along The Path Of Virtue Or One
Who Loves virtue and Piety, The most Forebearing.

In the Holy Quraan Allah the Creator says that he is different
from creation. If Allah the All Powerful, the Creator of everything
don't need what He has created? Muslims do your Creator need
your salaah, siyaam(pwosa), gadj? He created everything from
nothing or don't we believe that there is a Creator, do we believe
in our Imam's and Moulana's?

Now you get the smart people who will revere to the big band
theory.(Little do they know that the Holy Quraan even speaks
about that to.) I have one question for the clever people how can
order come from disorder?

Look at the car you drive, at your watch on your arm, look at your cell phone did anyone create these things? Then why don't we believe that there is a Creator?

So why did Allah create everything? Is it for us the most honoured creation men who have a brain to distinguish between right and wrong?
So lets use this brain and give credit to where credit is due to our Creator who created us to serve Him and no one else but Allah the One the Only firm Establish on the Thorn of Authority.

The holy Quraan says: "He said to the angels Bow down to Adam and they did except Satan he refused and haughty." Why would God command the angels to bow down to men? What does bow down mean in this context? Open your mind for a second or should I say be open minded for a second. Let us say bow down in this context means to serve. Does it mean that the angels serve us? Imagine that an angel bow down to you.
What does angel mean in this context or do we still believe what the white man has told us of how an angel looks and forget what the word angel mean, let us think out of the box here what if angel in this context means the sun, the trees, the earth, the water, the animals like the sheep, the cow, the chicken etc.

Let us look at the sun does it serve us? Do we need the sun to give us heat, do we need the sun to give us rain, do we need the sun to help the plants grow? Do we need the sun to give us time? What if the sun is an angel with 4 wings how about the sheep what do the sheep do for us, the sheep gives us food and give us wool for jackets and jerseys to keep us warm in the winter. So will we say the sheep serves two purposes to us and for that we give him 2 wings. How about the trees don't the trees that take our carbon-dioxide and turn if into fresh oxygen? But what does the humans do? We destroy those trees for money. Some trees gives us fruit, shade and fresh oxygen daily so shall we give the trees 3 wings?

If everything in the heavens, earth was created to serve men then how can a so called learned man still say on a Friday in his mosque: "give the jawoods, the kofaar the earth and the Muslims must wait for the heavens" isn't that a stupid statement?

How many Muslims believe that stupid statement almost like heaven is guaranteed for the Muslims.

So can you people see why it is hard to believe the Bible where it says that Satan wants to overthrow God almost like God is weak. Doesn't this line of the Holy Quraan make more sense, but let me get back to the Muslims and the part where Iblis says:" I am better then him: how many Muslims have that attitude today? How many Muslims think that they are better the other people, even better then other Muslims? How do you expect to enter heaven if you act like Iblis?
Didn't you learn anything from the way your prophet conducted his life, let me ask you this what made the people except Islam in the time of Mohammad (peach and blessings be upon him)? Was it the beard? Was it the thobe? Was it the sorbaan? Or was it none of the above?

If you but only knew and if you could only appreciate all the things your prophet went through, he was thrown with stones, he was called names, he was chased out of his place of birth but he didn't give up nor did he think he was better then people, he always acted better and learned us how to be a human. If Mohammad (peach and blessings be upon him) called the people to Islam through the way he conducted his life why do his so called followers believe today that the beard, the thobe, the sorbaan is part of there religion?

Let me do one better Mohammad (peach and blessings be upon him) said everything except the hands and face is ourah (needs to be covered) his followers says no that is a lie, Mohammad is a liar that's why they put there wife's and daughters in niqaab (covering of the face). Did you sell out your religion for customs? Isn't a woman who cover her ourah making a statement that she is concealing her sexuality but allowing her femininity to be brought out?

Lets take the 1st few verses of the Holy Quraan that was revealed to the prophet Mohammad (peach and blessings be upon him). Read (proclaim, investigate, study, go learn), in the name of your Lord and Cherisher Who created, Created man, from a clot of blood (fusion of the male and female cell), Proclaim and thy Lord is Most Bountiful, He who taught (how to use) the pen, taught men that which he knew not. Is this not that beautiful? Doesn't that answer a lot of questions? I have a question for the Muslims, If your Allah says he taught man what he knew not, and your Allah says that He is the all knowing.

How can you reject advancement (technology)? According to these verses knowledge comes from your Creator Allah so if you reject knowledge/advancement are you not rejecting part of your Holy Quraan? Don't even try to tell me that the knowledge that comes from a non Muslim you can't except because again I will tell you according to this verses your Creator taught man what he knows not.

What happened in the time of your Prophet (peach and blessings be upon him) after the battle of Badr? Didn't your prophet (peach and blessings be upon him) tell the non Muslims who were prisoners of war that if they taught 10 Muslims to read and

write they could get there freedom? So why are you rejecting
knowledge from a non Muslim? Do you think that you are better
then your Prophet?

How can you except technology by drive a new car with electric
windows, how can you use a computer with e-mail, a fax machine
but when it comes to your religion you reject it?

Is that not stupid, when it comes to your personal life you except technology
but when it comes to your religion you reject it.

According to your Holy Quraan you are suppose to lead the world in
advancement so why are you still trailing? Listen to what a non Muslim
professor from England who is a embryologist (who study the foetus
unborn baby). This man used the Holy Quraan for research and at the
end of his book he say do the Muslim know what they have in that holy
Quraan. So do you know what you have in that Holy Quraan?

Let me take you back in time to the battle of Safain where +_90000 Muslims
died where Ma'awia (aglil sunnie wal jamah) fought against the supporters
of Alie (shia's) so for years Muslim have fought against each other but let
me tell you the positive that came out of this battle Hercules the demi-god,
the son of zuz send his army to pick the bones of the Muslims in other
words to kill what was left but you know what happened, these to parties
stand together and defeated Hercules's army.

These two groups believe in the Holy Quraan and when THAT Holy
Quraan speaks about unity they stand together the Holy Quraan always
came 1st to them. Can the Muslims say the same today?

Look in Iraq today how the Shia's and the Aglil sunnies is killing each other
where is the Quraan where is unity?

Cant they learn anything from the Battle of Safain? Cant we look past our differences for once and look to what we all have in common? I do not care if you are a Shia, Aglil sunni wal jamah it is time to look past that and stop judging each other Is Allah not enough as a Judge? When will you Muslims go back to hold fast to the rope of your Creator? Or by the time are you lost?

Look what the Holy Quraan says that we are created from sperm so why do the people tell me that my origin is from an ape, have u looked at nature doesn't nature always repeat itself when you plant a apple seed does it not become an apple tree. When you wife is pregnant will she give birth to a baby or an ape?

So why don't we believe in a Creator anymore? When will we swallow our pride and submit to a Higher Power?

Let me tell what pride and technology did among the Muslims in Cape-Town for +_20years the Muslims where celebrating Eidul Adga (labarang gajie) 2 different days, for 20years there was a dispute about who was right. One group celebrated with Makkah and the other group said no we cannot celebrate with Makkah because our forefathers celebrate a day after Makkah. So the one group who celebrated a day after Makkah started rumours, calling the group who celebrated with Makkah names like mutazilah's (free thinkers) and the followers went along without investigating the truth. Little did the followers know what was the agreement that was made between the two groups but as the years went on the truth came out about who was wrong and who was right and do you know what happened?

Technology the radio station every year one the day of Eid you could hear how the people takbier(celebrating Eid). So the one group who celebrated a day after Makkah had to submit and had to celebrate with Makkah for one year but instead of apologies they continued with the name calling. Little did they know by calling the people of Majlisush Shura Al Islami mutazilah's they where given them compliments because most of them do not even know how and why the mutazilah's where created/started. So I will do you the favour and tell you.

During the later part of the first century, after the Hijrah, Abu Hassan Al Basri who died 110 after Hijrah he was a very eminent Muslim scholar who tried to bring the Muslims back to Islam. a student of Abu Hassan, named Wasil ibn Ata who died 113 after Hijrah differed with Abu Hassan on the issue of sin and repentance. An argument arose as to: what is the position of a perpetrator of a serious sin and he does not repent? According to the law, will such a person be regarded as an unbeliever? Wasil's view was that such a person is neither a believer nor an unbeliever.

This upset Abu Hassan as it was contrary to his views. Wasil thus broke away from the learning circle of Basri, together with a fellow-student Amr ibn Ubayd and together they formed the beginnings of a new group which became known as the mutazilah's. So what do we really know, we the followers of the different groups? We follow our leaders blindly without investigating the truth of the matter. How do we know that the leaders are not leading us straight into hell?

What do you in Cape-town really know about Majlisush Shura al Islami? Do we very take the time to find out what these people are standing for? If these people where right about Eid what other things are they still right about? Why are we so quick to judge?

Who knows maybe these people can learn us and our so called learned people more about the Holy Quraan. Or do we judge them because unlike us who is like parrots memorizing the Holy Quraan everyday these people study the Holy Quraan like it should be studied.

Why don't we give these people a chance to lead the Muslim Uma and see what they have to offer. If you study these people, if you sit in there madressa's (schools) or if you listen to there lectures on a Friday you will find that these people know what they are talking about. If there was degrees among the ulama you will find that these people whom you call names would all have doctors degrees and the rest who started this rumours have a degree in story telling.

Why when the learned people of Majlisush Shura Al Islami speaks on the radio someone always interfere and some how, some way they never get to come back for a second time? Are you afraid that these people might educate the Muslim Uma? Why don't we do what the learned people did in the past and debate?

This way the people will have the option to choose who's view they can follow. I am sure this way we will resolve many issues among the learned people.

But it is not my choice let the people of Cape-Town decide.

You can have a debate once a month maybe on live radio, on the internet and maybe on one of the television channels.

The west say that the Muslims don't give there women rights when it is there rappers that teaches the kids to disrespect women calling the bitches and whore's what I can't understand how can Mohammad (peach and blessings be upon him) give the animals rights but not their women?

When the Holy Quraan says respect your mothers. Do you have a mother? Do you have a sister? Will your sister be a mother?

Why do Islam say a woman must cover her body, is it to protect her? How many women are raped for the way that they dress themselves? Why cant a woman show her body off, if a woman is pregnant does she develop stretch marks? So ask that woman with stretch marks to walk around and show her body off.

How can Muslims not respect there woman when the women are the people who carry a nation or do the men give birth?

In Islam the man must look after there women, support them, make sure that all there needs are met. But in the second book we will discuss women rights in Islam in detail and proof all those people who have a degree in story telling wrong for saying that a woman have half a brain. What do you know about Islam?

How can people say you cannot be a free thinker when the Holy Quraan encourage free thinking Sura Alie Imraan" in the alteration of day and night is a sign for those who can think" how can the people say you cannot ask questions when the Holy Quraan encourage that you ask questions Sura Bakara "they are asking you about gayd (Mohammad)" So what do you know about Islam?

Is there any sunnan's in the fard salaah? Look at the tablieg jama they say that they are doing the work of the sagaba but every time when you hear them speak they quote out of a book called tablieg nisaab. Did the sagaba quote out of a book or did the sagaba use the Holy Quraan? How can you quote from a book that clashes with the Holy Quraan? How can you say that if I have a dog in my yard it scares away the angels? Is that not a stupid statement? Do you even know what Imam Gazalie, who was a great philosopher in Islam say about that gadith? Imagine that a dog who I keep to scare away burglars scares away angels.

So I have one question for the tablieg jama: "the angel of death that comes to take my roog (spirit) is that not the same angel that comes and take the spirit (roog) of my dog? Don't you know the Ganafia-or Malikie mathaab in Fiqh? What do you know about Islam?

Why when you Muslims go to the toilet, why do you use water? Is it to wash the bacteria off there private parts? Why do you Muslims use water for wudu? What do you know about Islam except what the media tells us do we ever try to find out more about Islam or about the Holy Quraan?

Why do Muslims pray 5 times a day at 5 different times? Is that to remind them of there Creator the all Mighty? What can the Muslims learn from that salaah and why 5 different times?

But as soon as the salaah is finish they forget the purpose of that salaah and they go back to there old self's forgetting about there middle salaah (the time between thur and asr, magrieb and isha etc.) How can we lead if we do not know how to follow?

Remember a few years back when the people appointed a new pope sum of the people was upset and outrage with his appointment. Do you remember that time? So what did the pope do to get the attention away from him? He attack the poor Muslims and there prophet Mohammad (peach and blessings be upon him) because he couldn't take the heat anymore. Well Mr. Pope if you can't take the heat get out of the kitchen. How can a respected spiritual leader do something like that?

How can he be a spiritual leader if he don't respect other religions? Mohammad (peach and blessings be upon him) would never have done what you did. How can you talk bad about a man who went through worst things then what you went through.

A man who I would give my life for, a man who was called a madman, one possessed by an evil spirit, a man who's people turned on him because of the message that he brought, a man who was laughed out in his face, when he walked in the road the people who did not believe in his message use to throw tied bundles of thorns with ropes of twisted palm-leafs and threw it cause him bodily harm, a man when he use to give over the message (preach) they made a noise so others could not listen to the message, they even threw the entrails of a goat on his back while he was performing pray and you want to make fun of that great man Mr. pope, a man who respected other people and there religion, a man who said even if they put the sun in my right hand and the moon in my left hand I would never give up my quest. Mr. pope if you knew anything about Islam or about the Holy Quraan you would know that the Muslims believe in Jesus the son of Mary and that there are even a chapter in the Holy Quraan that speaks about the birth of Jesus, about his life and about the so called crucifixion.

But it looks like you do not know anything or the only thing you know is how to insult a dead man and others religion. If you were half the man Mohammad (peach and blessings be upon him) was you would apologize to the Muslims and you would address the bible-scholars by answering the questions that they pose about the originality of the bible or do one better and address the movies like "Soulplane" who makes fun of your priests by showing them as gay man and "Stigmata" who say that your church is hiding some scriptures of the Holy Bible. So next time you open your mouth Mr. Pope know that there is someone who is listening who would fight for the truth because the truth shall set you free.

Before we get to the conclusion I just need to ask the Muslims a few last questions. Every year me'arage I hear the same story about how your prophet Mohammad (peach and blessings be upon him) after being in the presence of our Creator the Merciful and receiving the gift of salaah Mohammad (peach and blessings be upon him) went up and down for about 5times.

In this story you will find that the person sending him up and down is the prophet Moses. Two questions about this story in the Holy Quraan your Creator says that He the all Mighty never changes his laws here you will find a law was change 5 times. Question 2 the Holy Quraan says that your Creator is the all Knowing but here you will find that the prophet Moses knows more then your Creator. So tell me is the Holy Quraan wrong and who's prophet is Moosa? So did the jawood had a hand in this s scripture and how many other scriptures did they get to that to?

But who am I to say what you should believe when I am just a man trying to bring the Muslims back to the Holy Quraan and there old ways when they where still united and feared, in the time when they debated there issues and respected each others opinions when they could put there differences aside and look to the bigger picture (unity) when there ego's did not get in the way, in the time when they did not think they where prophets but there actions spoke to you as if they were prophets.

So when will that time ever come when the Muslims will unite again? When will the time come when the Muslims will look to the Holy Quraan for answer?

What I do not understand in the time of the Ghoelafa—ur—rasiedien(the imams after the dead of the prophet Mogammad s.a.w) the leaders of Islam these people were afraid to quote what the prophet Mogammad said but these days everybody who think he is a learned man or even a prophet are not afraid

to quite even thought half the stuff they quote are untrue it seems like they have forgotten what the prophet Mogammad said: "those who utter a lie against me his place will be in hell."

So how dare you Muslims speak ill about my prophet and say that he was bewitched by a jewish lady named Zainub bint Miscum, If that story is true then where was the protection of my Lord, the Great, the Eternal, my Protector Allah and you who believe that story then the verses that was revealed to the Prophet(s.a.w) in that time should be rejected.

How can you except that verses and my question to you is what makes you different from the people in the time of the prophet who said the same thing, because of the message the Prophet(s.a.w) conveyed?

If this was a movie you can call me the Avatar from the movie the Last Airbender, or I could be Keanon Reeves from the movie the Matrix and if this was a cartoon you can call me Goku Supersaint from Dragonball z. It is your choice to reject or to except and instead of wanting to burn the Holy Quraan take the time to read it because just maybe you would find wisdom in it.

Look at a few years back every body made fun of the Muslims about circumcision and today they are encouraging it.

CONCLUSION

In studying the religion of Islam and Christianity I you will find that these religions have plenty in common. Muslims except all prophets including Jesus the son of Mary with all the miracles he did I bet if you could proof to the Muslims when is the truth birthdate of Jesus they would celebrate it with you. The reason why muslims reject 25th December as the birthdate of Jesus because some of them say, that date was invented but the people who reject Jesus as a prophet, who calls him a bastard(someone who was conceived out of wedlock). So if this is true why do the Christians follow that date blindly?

So why do you want to burn the Holy Quraan when the Holy Quraan is the explanation of the 10 commandments in detail plus plenty more.

Did you know there are even some Muslims who believe that Jesus the son of Mary would come back . . . I just got it! The topic of the 1st debate between the Muslims. I can see it now The Return of Jesus the son of Mary.

Those who except his return against those who reject his return unless you are afraid to stand up for what you believe in?

To all the people do not believe everything you hear, make it your mission to find out for yourself what the truth is. If you are a Christian read the Holy Quraan that will not make you a Muslim. Who knows maybe you will find what you have been looking for.maybe you will find some answers.

Muslims respect all religions because in the time of the prophet Mogammad(s.a.w) when there was just 16 Muslims(12men and 4 women) who had to leave there birthplace to Abyssinia(which is called Ethiopia now) because they where hunted down by their own people for excepting Islam Christian King gave them a place to stay in his Christian land.

SAUDI-ARABIA

The Muslim land where all Muslims goes every year for a religious journey or spiritual up liftment in the time of Gajz or Umra(the birthplace of the prophet Mogammad s.a.w). Were they visit the holy Kaba that was build by the prophet Abraham and his son(so there you see another thing that the Muslims and Christians have in common) confirmed in the Holy Quraan all the other stories is false.

The centre of the universe a building that was build to unify the Muslims all over the world, a building were Muslims turn to when they perform there prayer 5 times a day. When you see that building for the 1st time it looks like something out of a movie and you ask yourself what makes this building so special, when you tawaaf around this special building all you can see is yourself leading prayer in this special place leading prayer for the people of Allah the Most Merciful who excepted the oneness of their Creator and believe there is no One Greater then the One you put your head on the ground for, and you see yourself entering this great building that was build on believe and watching how it looks inside and you see in the time of the prophet Mogammad(s.a.w) how the Muslims of that time fought to get that special building back to the hands of the Muslims and you finally understand why. As you pass the door of this great building you see a man waving at you, a man that only you can see, the man who comes to you in your dreams ever since you were at the age of 6, a tear drops down your cheek and you know there is no better feeling then the felling to worship your Creator, a Creator who meets you half way when you give one step towards Allah the One the Only He gives two steps towards you and you make dua(pray) that Allah the Giver of all things to open the eyes of the Muslims world wide to bring them back to the time when they were one, to the time when they debated there issues, to the time when they could swallow their pride and know that you are not attacking their believe but you are just trying to show them a better way, to a time when the Holy Quraan always came 1st.

To the time where people did not dress like and think that they are prophets but to the time when they acted like prophets.

To the time when Islam molded you and you did not mold Islam. To the time when people stood firm on the truth even if it was against themselves. To the time when they used Arafa to discuss the Global problems of Islam. To the time when Islam lead the world and the others followed. To the time when people was ready to die for Islam. To the time when Muslims were united and their armies was feared.

In this country the crime rate is like 1%, a country where you can sleep in the street, a country where you do not have to worry about being robbed, where do not have to worry about someone will brake in to your house or car, where cars do not need alarms, houses do not look like prisons with burglar bars all around.

When it comes to your last days in Makka as you are about to leave for Madina you go for your goodbye-tawaaf when the hardest thing is to say goodbye to a building and you ask yourself : "what spiritual value does this great building have?" Allahoe-Akbar so you do not say goodbye you say till we meet again but this time you want to go for Gajz because your Umra trip opened your eyes to many possibilities. Then you come to Madina the place where most of the battles took place the place where the greatest man that ever walked the face of this earth is buried.

When you see that place as you look through the golden gates you see the same man, the man who came to you in your dreams, the same man you saw waving at you when you tawaafed around the Holy Kaba, the man smiles at you and you smile back your heart feels at ease when you get to the outside you see people looking at you smiling at you almost like they could see there are something special about you.

You remember the 1st dream you ever had of this man when you walked beside him and you could see his footprints in the sand and you remember he told you something in a language you could not understand yet but now after this experience you finally know what the dream means, you finally understand what those words was that the man spoke to you and you tell yourself even if they put the son in my right hand and the moon in my left hand I will not give up this quest. So Muslims no matter how hard you fight against me I will fight you harder.

Don't you understand I owe my life to Allah the One Firm Established On The Throne Of Authority Islam made me who I am so now it is the time to give back to my religion. What have you done for your religion lately?

The Boys Life

I hate to be the bearer of bad news but somebody got to do it I just love my job. So tell me how do you stop someone who has an obsession with God his Creator? Someone who sees his Creator The Most Merciful in everything that he does? Someone who takes nothing for granted. Ask a blind man what is his biggest wish, what do you think his answer would be, to see? Ask someone in a wheelchair what is his biggest wish, will his answer be, to walk?

So why do so many people take the simple things for granted even their sleep when the Holy Quraan says Allah the Great created sleep as a mercy to man kind.

Someone who's best friend is himself, someone who gets lost in his own mind for minutes, hours, even days who believed if you want to be the best you should learn from the best that's why he is a student of Usuludin College in Cape Town.

The best place of Islamic education in the world at this point in time almost like Al Azar back in the 19th century.

Someone who is so crazy he puts a target on his own back. But this boy was not always like this let me tell you about the time when he was ANGRY at God And Mad at the World but for that you have to wait for the 2nd book . . . .